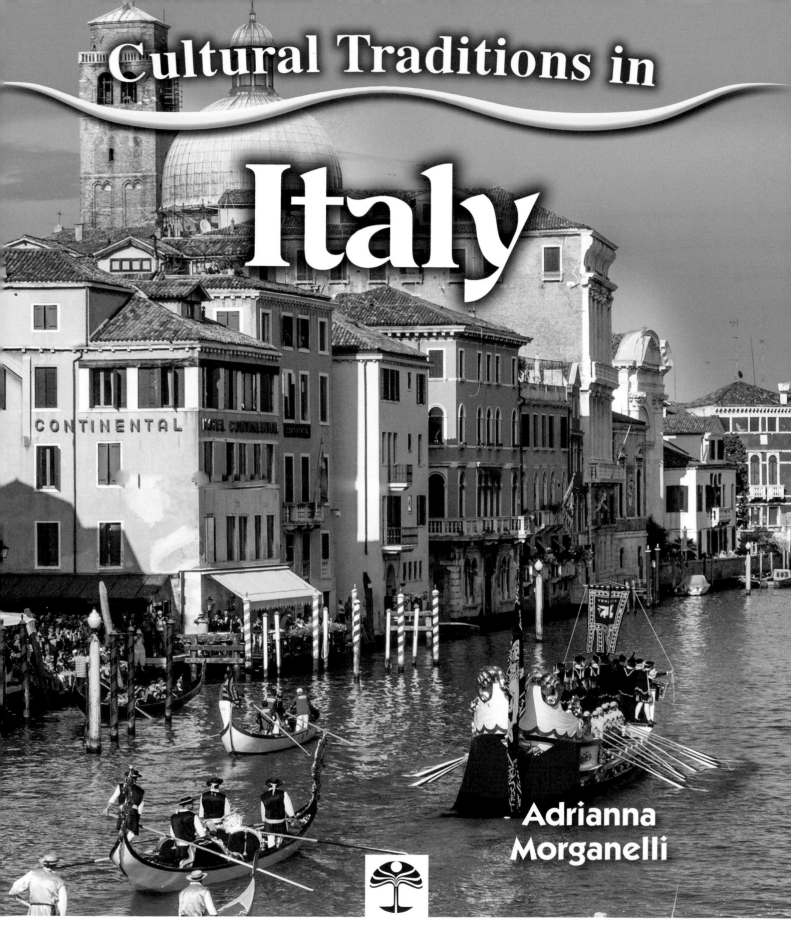

Cultural Traditions in

Italy

Adrianna
Morganelli

Crabtree Publishing Company
www.crabtreebooks.com

Crabtree Publishing Company
www.crabtreebooks.com

Author: Adrianna Morganelli

Publishing plan research and development:
 Reagan Miller

Editorial director: Kathy Middleton

Editors: Janine Deschenes, Crystal Sikkens

Proofreader and indexer: Petrice Custance

Photo research: Crystal Sikkens, Tammy McGarr

Designer: Tammy McGarr

Production coordinator and prepress technician:
 Tammy McGarr

Print coordinator: Katherine Berti

Cover: Model of Leonardo da Vinci's plan for a helicopter-like machine from 1493 (top left); Manuscript writing of Leonardo da Vinci (top); Person in costume celebrating Carnival in Venice (right); Various traditional Italian cookies (bottom right); Olive branch (bottom center); Wheel of Parmigiano-Reggiano cheese (bottom center); Murano glass candies (bottom left); Duomo cathedral in Florence (left)

Title page: The annual Regata Storica on Venice's Grand Canal.

Photographs:
Alamy: © Wead: p6; © Luigi de Pompeis: p10; © epa european pressphoto agency b.v.: p11 (top); © John Warburton-Lee Photography: p14; © PACIFIC PRESS: p17; © imageBROKER: p27; © Matthias Scholz: p29 (middle); © JMS: p30
Getty: Marco Secchi: p9
iStock: © jr2001: title page; © RiccardoChiades: p13 (bottom); © robyvannucci: p23
Keystone Press: © Antonio Masiello: p26
Public Domain: p7 (right); p29 (bottom)
Shutterstock: © Melodia plus photos: front cover (right); © Pecold: p15; © Eugenio Marongiu: p5; © MagSpace: p12 (top); © marchesini62: p12 (bottom); © Stefano Tinti: pp 16, 19 (top); © Maxim Tupikov: p18; © ROBERTO ZILLI: pp 20–21, 28; © marino bocelli: p22; © Rostislav Glinsky: p31 (bottom)
Superstock: Credit: Lynne Otter / age fotostock: pp24–25 (bottom)

All other images by Shutterstock

Library and Archives Canada Cataloguing in Publication

Morganelli, Adrianna, 1979-, author
 Cultural traditions in Italy / Adrianna Morganelli.

(Cultural traditions in my world)
Includes index.
Issued in print and electronic formats.
ISBN 978-0-7787-8087-8 (bound).--
ISBN 978-0-7787-8091-5 (paperback).--
ISBN 978-1-4271-8101-5 (html)

 1. Festivals--Italy--Juvenile literature. 2. Holidays--Italy--Juvenile literature. 3. Italy--Social life and customs--Juvenile literature. 4. Italy--Civilization--Juvenile literature. I. Title. II. Series: Cultural traditions in my world

GT4852.A2M67 2016   j394.26945   C2015-907457-6
                                      C2015-907458-4

Library of Congress Cataloging-in-Publication Data

Names: Morganelli, Adrianna, 1979- author.
Title: Cultural traditions in Italy / Adrianna Morganelli.
Description: New York, NY : Crabtree Publishing Company, [2016] | Series: Cultural traditions in my world | Includes index. | Description based on print version record and CIP data provided by publisher; resource not viewed.
Identifiers: LCCN 2015046327 (print) | LCCN 2015044048 (ebook) | ISBN 9781427181015 (electronic HTML) | ISBN 9780778780878 (reinforced library binding : alkaline paper) | ISBN 9780778780915 (paperback : alkaline paper)
Subjects: LCSH: Festivals--Italy--Juvenile literature. | Italy--Social life and customs--Juvenile literature.
Classification: LCC GT4852.A2 (print) | LCC GT4852.A2 M67 2016 (ebook) | DDC 394.26945--dc23
LC record available at http://lccn.loc.gov/2015046327

Crabtree Publishing Company

www.crabtreebooks.com   1-800-387-7650

Printed in Canada/022016/IH20151223

Copyright © **2016 CRABTREE PUBLISHING COMPANY.** All rights reserved. No part of this publication may be reproduced, stored in a retrieval system or be transmitted in any form or by any means, electronic, mechanical, photocopying, recording, or otherwise, without the prior written permission of Crabtree Publishing Company. In Canada: We acknowledge the financial support of the Government of Canada through the Canada Book Fund for our publishing activities.

Published in Canada
Crabtree Publishing
616 Welland Ave.
St. Catharines, ON
L2M 5V6

Published in the United States
Crabtree Publishing
PMB 59051
350 Fifth Avenue, 59th Floor
New York, New York 10118

Published in the United Kingdom
Crabtree Publishing
Maritime House
Basin Road North, Hove
BN41 1WR

Published in Australia
Crabtree Publishing
3 Charles Street
Coburg North
VIC 3058

Contents

Welcome to Italy!

Italy is a country located in southern Europe. It borders France, Switzerland, Austria, and Slovenia. Today, more than 60 million people live in the 20 regions that make up the country of Italy. The official language is Italian, but each region has its own **dialect**. Language is just one part of Italy's unique culture. The work of many important Italian **scholars**, artists, and scientists have also helped shape the culture of this country.

Did You Know?
Many Italians refer to their country as *lo Stivale*, which means "the Boot," because of the country's shape.

Religion is a big part of Italy's culture. Most Italians practice **Roman Catholicism**. Because of this, many of the country's celebrations, festivals, and customs are based on Roman Catholic beliefs. There are small groups of Italians that practice other religions such as **Islam** and **Hinduism**. These people celebrate important events based on their religions.

These **Muslims** in Milan, Italy, are celebrating the last day of Ramadan. Ramadan is a month-long Islamic holiday that consists of prayer and **fasting**.

Feast Days of Patron Saints

In the Catholic Church, different **patron saints** are considered to be advocates, or supporters, for specific people, animals, places, or professions and crafts, such as bakers, butchers, or basket-makers. Each patron saint has a holiday, known as a feast day, dedicated to them. Believers remember and celebrate the saint on that day.

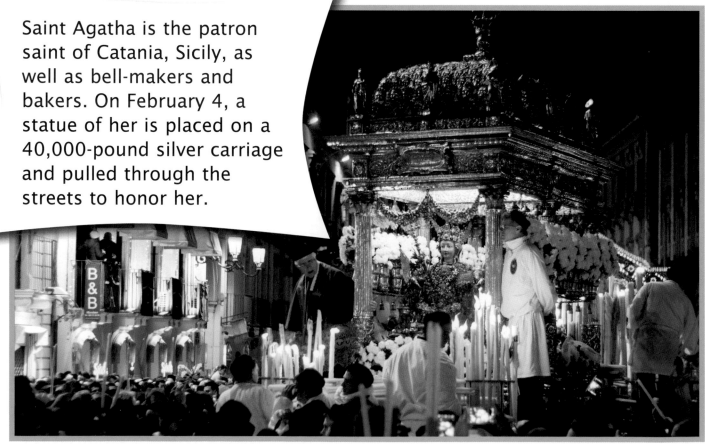

Saint Agatha is the patron saint of Catania, Sicily, as well as bell-makers and bakers. On February 4, a statue of her is placed on a 40,000-pound silver carriage and pulled through the streets to honor her.

Many countries have patron saints. Italy's two patron saints are Saint Francis of Assisi and Saint Catherine of Siena. Italian cities and towns also have their own local patron saints. This is often the place where the patron saints were born or did their life work. Each city or town has a local holiday dedicated to their patron saint.

Saint Francis of Assisi is also the patron saint of animals and the environment. His feast day is October 4.

Saint Catherine of Siena is also the patron saint of protection against fire and illness. Her feast day is April 29.

The New Year

In Italy, there are many parties that celebrate the beginning of a New Year, or *il capodanno*. In cities such as Rome, Milan, Bologna, Palermo, and Naples, people attend huge outdoor shows featuring bands, dancing, and midnight fireworks displays. Parties last until sunrise so that people can watch the first sunrise of the New Year.

Fantastic fireworks are displayed over Republic Square, in Rome, on New Year's Eve.

A fun tradition on New Year's Day is to take a dip in the freezing water at the Venice Lido beaches.

Did You Know?
One New Year's custom includes throwing one's old things out the window to symbolize acceptance of new things to come. Many people also wear red underwear on New Year's Day to bring good luck.

On New Year's Eve, Italian families and friends share a feast. Lentils are eaten because they symbolize money and good fortune. A spicy pork sausage called *cotechino* is also eaten. Italians believe eating pork welcomes a richness of life in the coming year. They toast to a new year with Italian sparkling wines called *spumante* and *prosecco.*

Epiphany

Each year on January 6, Italians celebrate the Epiphany. The Epiphany **commemorates** the arrival of the three **Wise Men** at the birthplace of Jesus Christ, who Christians believe is the son of God. The Wise Men brought gifts for the baby Jesus, and because of this, the Epiphany is the main day for giving gifts to one another.

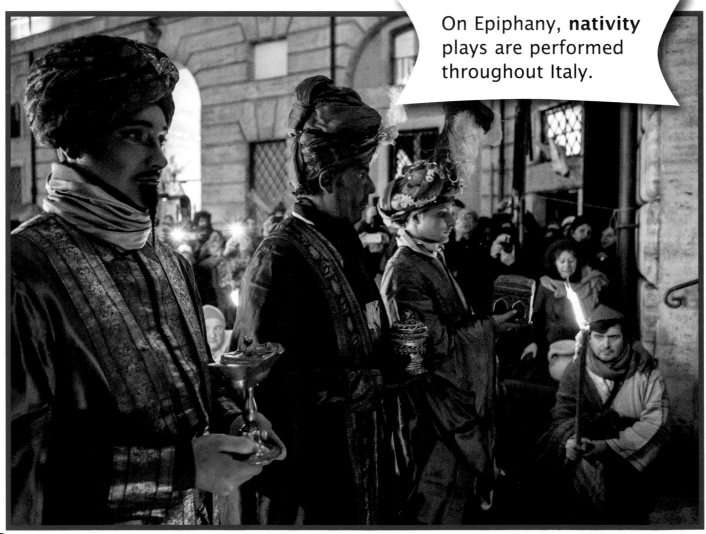

On Epiphany, **nativity** plays are performed throughout Italy.

In Venice, men dress as La Befana and race their boats on the Grand Canal in the *Regatta della Bafane*, or Befana races.

Italy's celebration of the Epiphany includes a legend of a witch known as La Befana. Italians say that on January 5, La Befana flies from home to home on her broomstick bringing gifts to children. On this night, children hang stockings for La Befana to fill with candy and toys.

Many people have decorations of La Befana in their home.

Carnival

Forty days before Easter, a huge winter festival called Carnival is celebrated in Italy. This fun-filled party lasts several weeks, and is marked by parades with giant floats, people dressed in elaborate costumes and masks, firework displays, music, and dancing.

Venice is famous for making the most beautiful and elaborate Carnival masks.

One of the biggest Carnival parades is held in the city of Viareggio in northern Tuscany.

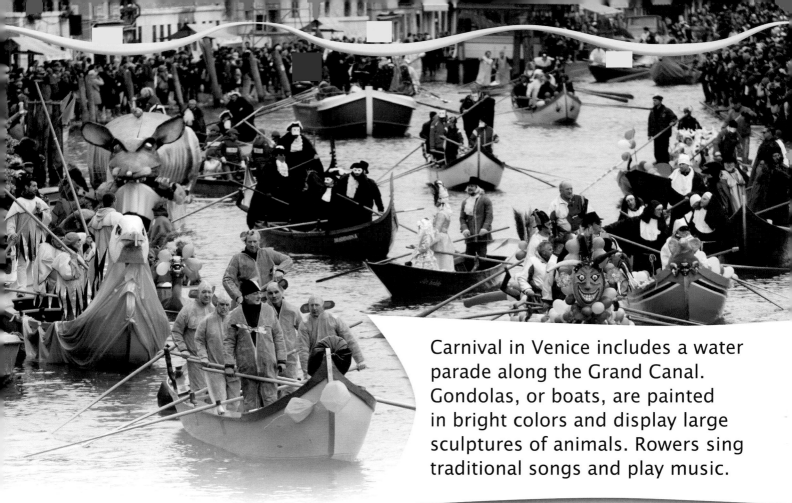

Carnival in Venice includes a water parade along the Grand Canal. Gondolas, or boats, are painted in bright colors and display large sculptures of animals. Rowers sing traditional songs and play music.

Italy's largest food fight takes place during Carnival! In the town of Ivrea, in Piedmont, thousands of people gather in the center of town for an orange-throwing battle. The participants are divided into nine teams. Spectators wear special red hats called *berretto frigio* for protection, and to show that they are not battling.

Some spectators still get hit with oranges that have missed their targets!

Easter

Easter, or *Pasqua*, is one of the most beloved holidays in Italy. It often falls in April. Several religious **processions** are held on the days leading up to Easter Monday. Statues of Jesus and his mother, the Virgin Mary, are paraded through cities, and are displayed in the main squares of towns.

A 24-hour procession known as the *Misteri de Trapani* in Trapani, Sicily, has been held on Good Friday since the 1600s. The procession features 20 wooden floats and canvas statues that display scenes about Jesus Christ.

On Easter Monday, many people attend mass. Families and friends then gather at dances, concerts, and to play games. Children are given hollow chocolate eggs that have gifts hidden inside. A large feast is shared, and traditional foods such as lamb, goat, and artichokes are enjoyed. Special Easter breads, as well as a pie-like dessert called *pastiera*, are also eaten on Easter Monday.

Did You Know?
A **nun** who lived in Naples first created the *pastiera*. She wanted to make a dessert to celebrate Spring. Later, the nuns began to make batches of *pastiera* for the rich families in Naples.

On Easter Sunday in Florence, a cart loaded with fireworks is pulled by oxen to the cathedral square. It is believed that a successful fireworks display will guarantee a successful harvest, business, and everyday life.

Liberation Day

Some holidays in Italy have been established to honor the freedom of the Italian people. Each year on April 25, Italians celebrate Liberation Day. This holiday commemorates the liberation, or freedom, of the Italian people from leader Benito Mussolini and the German **Nazi occupation** during World War II.

On Liberation Day, thousands of people take part in parades to remember the end of Mussolini's rule of Italy.

Each year on Liberation Day, the Italian military band performs at the Quirinale Square, in Rome.

On this day, people remember the Italians who fought against Mussolini and the Germans as part of the group known as the Italian Resistance. Marches and parades are held throughout Italy to honor the soldiers and civilians who died during the war.

Did You Know?
Benito Mussolini ruled Italy from 1922 to 1943. His 21 years as Prime Minister ended when public opinion turned against him. He was voted out of office, then arrested and executed.

Labor Day

Labor Day, or May Day, is celebrated on May 1. It is an important day in Italy that commemorates the worker. Labor Day, or *Festa del Lavoro*, is a public holiday, and workplaces and schools are closed.

On Labor Day, many people organize protests to improve the conditions of workers in Italy.

Many people dress in various work-related costumes to take part in the Labor Day parades.

The beaches in Italy are usually filled with locals on Labor Day. Many people also attend parades, festivals, and concerts. One major concert is the *Concerto del Primo Maggio* held in Rome. Many famous bands and songwriters perform at the concert, and it is broadcast live on television.

Republic Day

Another Italian holiday that celebrates freedom is Republic Day, which is on June 2 each year. Republic Day celebrates the establishment of an Italian republic and the abolishment, or end, of the monarchy on June 2, 1946. A republic is a form of government in which the people elect, or choose, the leaders that will represent them.

Italians celebrate Republic Day by watching parades, fireworks, concerts, and sharing picnics with family and friends. Each year, a wreath is laid at the Tomb of the Unknown Soldier in Rome. The tomb was completed in 1924, and has an eternal flame. It was built to honor all of Italy's fallen soldiers.

On Republic Day, members of the Italian Army take part in military parades.

Assumption of Mary

Ferragosto, also known as the Assumption of Mary, is a national holiday that is celebrated on August 15. On this day, Catholics celebrate Mary's acceptance into Heaven. They consider this a symbol of Jesus's promise that all Christians will be received into Heaven when they die.

Did You Know?
The *Festa dei Candelieri* is a festival held on *Ferragosto* in Sardinia. Many games are played, including a race that features teams of men carrying large heavy candles.

On *Ferragosto*, people celebrate with parades, and many pray to the Virgin Mary in churches. Processions of people carry statues of the Virgin Mary down the streets of towns and cities.

Italians like to vacation at the beach for *Ferragosto*, so the coast becomes very crowded, and many cities become empty of people. Some places like to celebrate with festivals. In Rome, people celebrate the *Gran Ballo di Ferragosto*, or the Grand Ball of *Ferragosto*. Each square in the city has music and people performing different types of dance. Huge fireworks displays can be seen in Liguria and Cappelle sul Tavo, on the Abruzzo coast.

Artists create beautiful chalk drawings on the churchyard of Santa Maria delle Grazie, in the town of Varallo. On Assumption Day, hundreds of people gather to look at the artwork, which honors the Virgin Mary.

All Saints' and All Souls' Days

Each year on November 1, Italians celebrate a national holiday called All Saints' Day. On this day, people honor all the saints who have died for the Catholic Church. Many believe there is a spiritual connection between those in Heaven and those who are living.

On All Saints' Day, people visit the graves of deceased relatives and friends. They clean the gravestones, and leave lighted candles and flowers.

24

The following day, November 2, is considered a day of prayer and remembrance for all people who have died. This day is called All Souls' Day. Many people believe that their deceased loved ones will visit them, so they engage in traditions to welcome them home. For example, in Trentino Alto Adige, people ring bells to call the dead to their homes. They set a place for them at their tables, and keep their fireplaces burning throughout the night.

Pan dei morti is a traditional Italian cake eaten on All Souls' Day.

Did You Know?
On All Souls' Day in Veneto, people give their loved ones special cookies called *ossi da morti*, or bones of the dead.

Feast of the Immaculate Conception

According to the Catholic Church, God made the Virgin Mary immaculate, or free from sin or wrong-doing, when she was conceived, or created inside her mother. To honor this event, most Italians celebrate the Feast of the Immaculate Conception every year on December 8.

On this holiday, Pope Francis, the head of the Catholic Church, leads a special ceremony at a place known as the Spanish Steps, in Rome.

Throughout Italy, people attend parades, fireworks, processions through the streets, and special church masses on this holiday. In Abruzzo, the Feast of the Immaculate Conception is celebrated with bonfires and singing traditional songs. Although the Feast of the Immaculate Conception is a national holiday, many shops are open for people to begin their Christmas shopping.

Many stores sell goods related to the Virgin Mary, including paintings and statues.

Christmas

Christmas in Italy is a joyous celebration. On Christmas Eve, families gather for a special meal called *Fiesta dei Sette Pesci*, which means Feast of the Seven Fishes. The meal is typically made up of seven seafood dishes. Families then attend midnight mass together. The most popular mass is given by the Pope at Saint Peter's Basilica, in Vatican City.

Did You Know?
In Umbria, near the top of Mount Ingino, an enormous Christmas tree stands more than 2,000 feet (650 meters) tall. It is decorated with more than 700 lights, and is topped with a star that can be seen for 31 miles (50 km).

Houses are decorated with lights, Christmas trees, and **nativity** scenes. Nativity scenes also decorate churches and outdoor squares, such as this one in Castello Square, Turin.

On Christmas Day, children awake to find that *Babbo Natale*, or Father Christmas, has left gifts for them beneath their Christmas trees. The Pope delivers a special Christmas message from the window of his apartment overlooking Saint Peter's Square. Italian families share a feast made up of meats, pastas, and traditional desserts including *pannetone*, a sweet bread loaf made with chocolate, candied fruit, or raisins.

In Umbria, canoeists dressed as *Babbo Natale* sail along the river in canoes decorated with lights to give gifts to children along the shore.

The Christmas Day meal in Italy usually includes a popular dessert called *struffoli*. *Struffoli* are fried balls of dough drizzled with honey, cinnamon, and bits of orange rind.

Food Festivals

Throughout Italy, festivals are held to celebrate Italians' love for their traditional foods, such as artichokes, white asparagus, chestnuts, and olive oil. At each festival, restaurants serve special meals that highlight the celebrated food, and people take part in crafts, music, and dancing.

Did You Know?
In recent years, the Eurochocolate festival in Perugia, features an igloo made from 8,000 pounds (3,629 kg) of chocolate bricks!

In Perugia, about one million people gather to celebrate chocolate at the Eurochocolate festival in mid-October. People sample chocolates from around the world, watch street performances, and participate in chocolate-sculpting contests.

Northern and central Italy have some of the largest truffle festivals. Truffles are a kind of mushroom. The festivals are usually held in October and November, which is the season for gathering truffles. The Alba International White Truffle Fair in Alba, Italy, is one of the largest truffle festivals. Visitors to the fair can attend concerts, the White Truffle market, wine tastings, a donkey race, and sample many recipes that feature the truffle.

White truffles.

The White Truffle Fair in Alba also features shows and a parade with people dressed in 13th century clothing. These performers act out parts of Alba's history.

Glossary

commemorate To honor

dialect A variety of a language that is characteristic of a particular area or group of people

fast To abstain from eating food

Hinduism A religion or way of life, most notably found in India and Nepal

Islam The religious faith of Muslims based on the teachings of the prophet Muhammad

monarchy A form of government whereby the ruler is a sovereign, such as a king, queen, or emperor

Muslim Someone who practices the religion of Islam

nativity A depiction of the birth of Jesus, celebrated at Christmas

Nazi A member of, or a believer in the ideas of, the German political party led by Adolf Hitler from 1933 to 1945

nun A woman who devotes her life to doing religious work

occupation To take over an area by military force

patron saint A saint whom Roman Catholics regard as the advocate of a nation, craft, or activity

procession A group of people walking in a ceremonial manner

Roman Catholicism The faith and practice of the Roman Catholic Church based on the teachings of Jesus Christ

scholar Someone who is very knowledgeable in a particular subject

Wise Men The three men who visited Jesus bearing gifts after his birth

Index